Editor
Laura Fransella
Picture Research
Jenny Golden
Production
Eva Wrennall
Teacher Panel
Pat Kaye
Shimon Levison
Roy Williams
Consultant
John W. R. Taylor
Illustrators
Gordon C. Davies/Linda Rogers Associates
Lesley Passey/Linda Rogers Associates
Tony Payne

Published in the United
States by Silver Burdett
Company, Morristown, N.J.
1980 Printing

ISBN 0 382 06392 9

Library of Congress
Catalog Card No. 80-50960

Photographic Credits
Aerofilms 37; Associated
Press 35; Decca Radar 34;
Nicholas Denbow 28; A. J.
Jackson 22; Philip Jarrett
9; Lufthansa German
Airlines 36 (right), 38, 39
(bottom) 42; Popperfoto
19; Radio Times Hulton
Picture Library 18
(bottom), 20; Peter
Shephard 41, 43;
Spectrum Colour Library
39 (top), 40; ZEFA UK Ltd
Günter Heil 33 (top), 36
(left); Zeppelin Museum,
Friedrichshaven 18 (top).

Air Travel

A. J. Jackson

Macdonald Educational

Contents

How to use this book
This book traces the history of air travel from the first balloons to Concorde and beyond. Look first at the contents page to see if the subject you are looking for is listed. For example, if you want to find out how an aeroplane flies, turn to page 26. The index on page 46 shows you the pages where a particular subject is mentioned and also whether it is illustrated. The glossary explains some of the new terms found in this book that are shown in the text in *italics*.

Dreams come true

People have probably dreamed of flying since prehistoric times and many envied birds their ability to fly. According to a Greek legend, Daedalus and his son Icarus escaped from a tower in Crete using feathered wings stuck together with wax. However, Icarus flew too near the sun, the wax melted and he plunged to his death.

Many other unfortunate 'birdmen' were killed or injured when they made wings for themselves and then jumped off high towers. A monk called Oliver broke both legs after launching himself from the top of Malmesbury Abbey in 1020. Clumsy flapping-wing machines called ornithopters were developed from about 1500, to help men try to fly. Several were designed by the Italian artist Leonardo da Vinci but the machines were never successful.

Balloons

In the 18th century, the dream of flying first came true. In France, the Mont-golfier brothers filled a large balloon

Above: a Montgolfier hot-air balloon carrying two passengers over Paris in 1783. The air was heated by a brazier of hot straw.

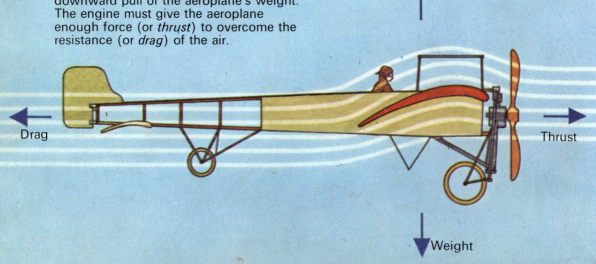

Below: the four basic forces which act on an aeroplane so that it can fly. The lift of the wings has to overcome the downward pull of the aeroplane's weight. The engine must give the aeroplane enough force (or *thrust*) to overcome the resistance (or *drag*) of the air.

Lift

Drag

Thrust

Weight

Otto Lilienthal with one of his hang gliders.

with hot air and made it rise into the air. The first flight with two men carried on a gondola underneath took place in 1783. Later in the same year two other Frenchmen made a flight in a hydrogen-filled balloon. Hydrogen is fourteen times lighter than air and gave the balloon far more 'lift'. Ballooning became very popular, but few long-distance flights were successful.

Gliders

In 1853, the first man-carrying glider was flown. A glider is a craft without an engine that stays in the air by soaring on air currents. It has to be launched by being towed, just as a kite is first pulled along the ground. From 1891, the German Otto Lilienthal made over 2,000 flights in his hang gliders before he died after a flying accident in 1896.

The first powered flight

Gliders could not make long flights without power but the engines of the time were far too heavy to be used. After many experiments, the American brothers Wilbur and Orville Wright fitted a glider with a light petrol engine and managed to fly for 36.5 metres in December 1903. It was the world's first powered and controlled flight.

Below: Orville and Wilbur Wright just before their first flight, at Kitty Hawk, North Carolina in December 1903.

First passenger flights

The Wright Brothers' *Flyer* was a *biplane*, which is an aircraft with two wings, one over the other. Most early machines were biplanes as two pairs of wings braced together were stronger than one. Modern aircraft are *monoplanes*, with only one main wing across the body.

There were more aviation pioneers after the Wright Brothers such as Alberto Santos-Dumont, a Brazilian, who flew a distance of 220 metres in 1906 and A V Roe who flew briefly for 30 metres at Brooklands in Surrey in 1908. S F Cody covered 426 metres at Farnborough later in the same year. However, these primitive aircraft and their pilots flew only a few metres above the ground.

By 1910, some aircraft were able to lift a second person crouching beside or behind the pilot. Both were in the open, holding tight as the air rushed past at about 80 km per hour. In 1911, a Frenchman called Roger Sommer flew a biplane carrying five passengers for over an hour.

An aeroplane with passenger seats

By 1912, so many people wanted to try the experience of flying that most new aircraft had two seats. There were long queues for flights at the new flying-grounds. In 1913, the Grahame-White company built a big 120 hp (121 cv) Charabanc which carried as many as 10 passengers on rows of wicker seats for short-distance flights.

Below: a Blackburn Kangaroo of 1919 with the pilot sitting in an open cockpit.

Above: the pilot and passenger in a Henry Farman biplane. You can see both the engine and the propeller behind them.

Aircraft in wartime

Aircraft were used for combat for the first time during the First World War. France, Britain and Germany developed the first real bombers and fighters for attack and defence and passenger aircraft gained very much from the technical discoveries made during wartime.

Flying in bombers

There was no civilian flying in Europe during the war but short pleasure flights began again in 1919. People flew in aeroplanes that were no longer needed by the Royal Air Force. Dark green Handley Page and Blackburn Kangaroo bombers carried four or five passengers at a time over London from airfields in Cricklewood and Hendon.

Passengers found flights in these converted bombers very exciting. They flew standing up, in an open cockpit behind the wings. Within a year, tens of thousands of people had flown, taking off from meadows, airfields and even beaches. Some of the early aircraft used for pleasure flights were *seaplanes* or flying-boats that took off from the water at seaside resorts.

Airliners are born

As passenger aircraft developed from wartime bombers, there were the first attempts at starting regular air services. The Frenchman Louis Blériot had been the first pilot to fly across the English Channel, in 1909, but regular air services between England and France did not start until ten years later. In August 1919, a D.H.16 converted bomber carried four passengers to Paris. They had to travel in a tiny box-like space, shut in under a transparent lid. The first real airline service in the world ran for a few weeks in 1914 in the USA. Flying-boats were used to carry passengers the 35 km from Tampa to St Petersburg, in Florida.

Early flying conditions

Most early flights were in draughty open-cockpit machines from which the guns had been removed. Passengers had to wear helmets, goggles and leather coats to keep warm and in winter, many clutched hot water bottles! They suffered from air-sickness and from nerves. Air turbulence, noise and vibrations made flying very uncomfortable.

By the early 1920s, British, French, German, Swiss, Dutch, Belgian and Australian airlines had passenger aircraft but in the USA, long-distance aircraft at first carried only mail and not passengers.

Airliners with cabins

Airliners with cabins designed specially for passengers were used from 1919. In Germany, a Junkers all-metal monoplane was built, while in England, the D.H.18, the first British purpose-built passenger aircraft came into use. Eight people, seated on canvas seats, could be

Below: the Frenchman Louis Blériot was the first person to fly an aeroplane across the English Channel.

flown to Paris in two and a half hours; the journey had previously taken a whole day by boat and train.

By 1920, there were five flights daily by Instone Air Line to Paris, but only when the weather was fine. Sometimes, the airline's two-engined Vickers Vimy Commercial was used. This seated ten passengers in wicker chairs in a fat, oval cabin. The aircraft was called *City of London* and it was the largest and most famous of the early cross-Channel airliners. It took three hours to fly from London to Paris and was therefore slower than the D.H.18s.

Right: a German couple about to make a passenger flight in a converted bomber in 1919. Notice their helmets, goggles and thick coats. Their tightly-clasped hands show how nervous they must have been.

Below: the Vickers Vimy Commercial *City of London* on a flight from Croydon Aerodrome, to Paris.

Wings across the world

Above: Amy Johnson, the first woman to make a solo flight to Australia.

Above: Sir Alan Cobham, who charted many new airways.

The first air routes were quite short and mainly joined the chief cities of Europe. Many airmen were more ambitious, however, and wanted to fly across continents and oceans.

The first long flights

In 1919, the Australians Ross and Keith Smith were first to make the longest flight ever attempted. In turn frozen by the cold, tossed by storms, stuck in mud on flooded airfields and blistered by the sun, they flew 17,900 km from England to Australia in 28 days in a Vickers Vimy bomber.

Preparing for long air routes

In 1925, the long-distance pilot Alan Cobham set off in a small blue biplane to map all the landing grounds between Cairo and Cape Town. In 1926, he flew from Rochester to find the best route to Australia. He had replaced the wheels of his biplane by floats so that he

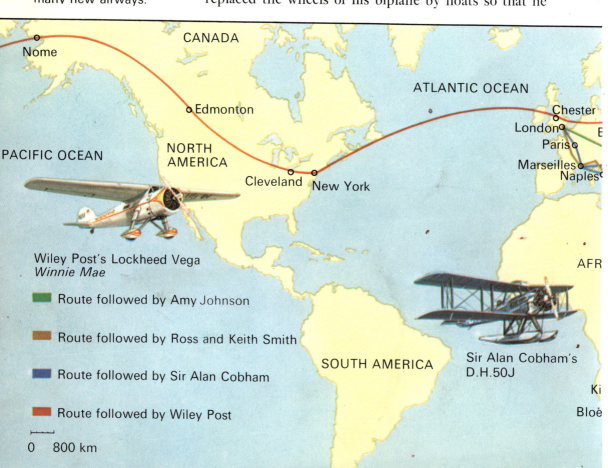

Wiley Post's Lockheed Vega
Winnie Mae

███ Route followed by Amy Johnson

███ Route followed by Ross and Keith Smith

███ Route followed by Sir Alan Cobham

███ Route followed by Wiley Post

0   800 km

Sir Alan Cobham's
D.H.50J

could take off and land on water. He was knighted after his return for his skill as a pilot.

Lone fliers

Many other pilots felt a similar spirit of adventure. An Australian called Bert Hinkler made the first solo flight from London to Darwin in $15\frac{1}{2}$ days in 1928. The first woman to make the solo flight was the Englishwoman Amy Johnson in her Gipsy Moth *Jason*. Her journey in 1930 took 19 days. In 1936, she flew a Percival Gull from London to Cape Town and back, taking less than eight days for the round trip! This was another major achievement.

Round the world

These lone pilots and their flights showed how reliable aircraft were becoming. People were beginning to think that flying was not as dangerous as they had imagined. Pilots of some airlines were even dreaming of a route right round the world and in 1931, an American called Wiley Post proved it possible. He circled the globe in eight and a half days in his monoplane *Winnie Mae*.

Above: Ross and Keith Smith, who flew from London to Darwin.

Above: Wiley Post, the first pilot to fly round the world.

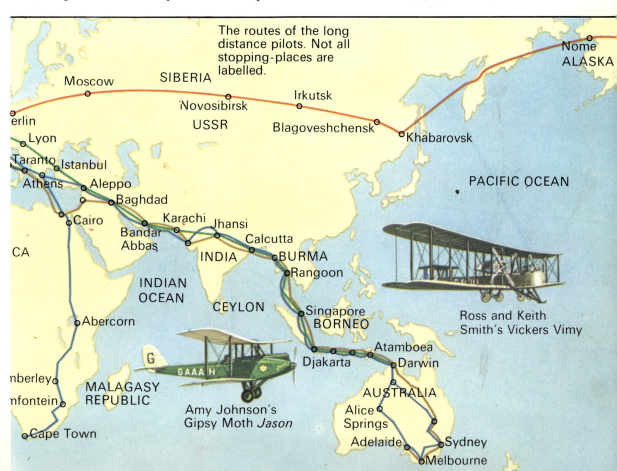

The routes of the long distance pilots. Not all stopping-places are labelled.

Nome
ALASKA

Moscow
SIBERIA
Irkutsk
Novosibirsk
erlin
Lyon
USSR
Blagoveshchensk
Khabarovsk
Taranto Istanbul
Athens Aleppo
Baghdad
PACIFIC OCEAN
Cairo
Karachi Jhansi
Bandar
Abbas
Calcutta
CA
INDIA
BURMA
Rangoon
INDIAN
OCEAN
CEYLON
Abercorn
Singapore
BORNEO
Ross and Keith
Smith's Vickers Vimy
nberley
Atamboea
Djakarta
Darwin
MALAGASY
REPUBLIC
nfontein
G
GAAA H
AUSTRALIA
Amy Johnson's
Gipsy Moth *Jason*
Alice
Springs
Cape Town
Adelaide
Sydney
Melbourne

World airlines begin

Fifty years ago, some European countries, particularly Britain, Belgium, the Netherlands, France and Italy controlled colonies and territories overseas. People who worked there needed to travel quickly and the airline companies began long-distance flights along the trails blazed by the lone pilots. In 1929, Imperial Airways began services from London to Karachi, which was then in India, and in 1931 flights started to Cape Town. The Dutch airline KLM started flights to Batavia, which is now Djakarta, in the Far East and Air France opened a route from Paris to Dakar in West Africa. The Belgian airline Sabena began flights to the Belgian Congo (now Zaire) in Africa and the German airline Lufthansa connected Berlin with Teheran in Iran.

Flights in the USA

Boeing Air Transport and National Air Transport, which later became United Air Lines, began a 4,200 km mail and passenger service in the USA in 1927. It spanned the country from the Atlantic to the Pacific Ocean. The trans-continental flights took 33 hours and the aircraft made 14 stops.

Flying conditions improve

The airliners that flew in the 1930s could carry about 15 passengers and flights gradually became more comfortable. Some cabins were furnished a little like railway carriages and had heating and ventilation. Light meals were served during the journey by a steward who stored food, cutlery, crockery and thermos flasks of coffee in a pantry at the rear of the cabin.

Long flights often took several days, however. (It took a week to fly to India.) Airfields were needed along the routes to provide petrol and servicing for the airliners and over-night accommodation for the passengers.

Long-distance aircraft

Most aircraft had three engines but could fly on two if one broke down. Biplanes were still used for long journeys, particularly Calcutta flying-boats which crossed the Mediterranean Sea and Hercules biplanes for longer flights beyond Cairo to India or South Africa. KLM, however, flew high-wing Fokker monoplanes to the Far East. From 1930, flights across the USA were by high-wing Ford Trimotors and later, Boeing biplanes of United Air Lines, seating 18 passengers, were used.

Below: a Fokker VII 3m monoplane of KLM (Royal Dutch Airlines) in 1929.

Above: an all-metal Ford Trimotor, as used for transcontinental flights in the United States after 1930.

Below: a three-engined Junkers Ju 52, used by the German airline Deutsche Lufthansa for long-distance flights in the 1930s.

Below: a British-built Short Calcutta flying-boat which was used on Imperial Airways' routes across the Mediterranean Sea.

Fast and streamlined

Above: a diagram to show a flat sloping surface producing a little lift as it moves through the air. It causes eddies which lessen the lift. Curved surfaces are now used instead.

Above: a diagram to show the circular end of a straight rod as it passes through the air. Eddies formed behind the rod try to hold it back. This is called air resistance, or drag.

In the 1930s, people who could afford it used air travel in place of journeys by rail and sea but air travel was still beyond the means of most ordinary people. Larger aircraft were needed. One of the most famous of these was the four-engined H.P.42 biplane owned by Imperial Airways, which carried 38 passengers on European routes. Another version of the H.P.42 with 24 seats carried passengers and mail beyond Cairo to Africa and India. The H.P.42s were far more comfortable inside than any previous airliner. There was room to move about and the cabins were sound-proofed. They could cruise at a speed of about 160 km per hour and were far more stable in the air than earlier airliners, which reduced airsickness.

Most aircraft used in the 1930s were still biplanes because two pairs of wings braced together with supports and wires were far stronger than one pair, and could lift heavier loads. However, the large wing area meant that there was increased *drag* or air resistance as the aircraft flew. This air resistance slowed them down.

Below: a Handley Page H.P.42 biplane of Imperial Airways. Different versions of this aircraft flew from 1931 to 1939 throughout Europe as well as to Africa and India. The H.P.42 was not only more comfortable than earlier airliners but was also extremely safe. It was called 'not an aeroplane but a legend'.

Passenger monoplanes

Aircraft designers thought that if the wing on a monoplane could be made strong enough to need no extra supports, air resistance would be greatly reduced and the aircraft would be able to fly at a higher speed. Several large monoplanes were built to test this theory. One of the first was the German four-engined Junkers G38 which flew for Lufthansa from 1929 to 1939. It had windows in the wing where some passengers could actually sit.

Strong light metal alloys were not yet available and the wings of a monoplane could only be made strong enough if they were also enormously thick. There was then a great deal of drag from the air and the new monoplanes were almost as slow as the biplanes had been. A Russian eight-engined monoplane flown in 1934 could carry 40 passengers and 23 crew but could cruise only at 218 km per hour.

The start of modern streamlined aircraft

In 1933, an American aircraft was built in an entirely new way. The Boeing 247 monoplane had a body which was streamlined; it was designed to slip through the air as easily as a fish through water, with the minimum of air resistance. It had thin but strong wings made out of new and improved metals. The pilot could wind up the undercarriage and its landing wheels and retract it behind the engines after take-off. This cut out the drag of the undercarriage wheels and supports and helped to increase speed. From 1935, airlines all over the world bought fleets of the Douglas DC-3 which could carry 28 passengers and cruise at 300 km per hour. Aircraft could now both travel fast and carry heavy loads.

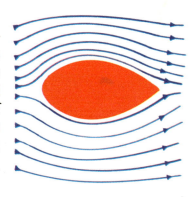

Above: a diagram to show how drag is reduced as much as possible by streamlining the shape of the body of an aircraft and any outside struts or supports. If these are blunt in front and taper at the rear, the air streams smoothly round each side without causing much drag.

Below: a Douglas DC-3, one of the first of the new all-metal streamlined aircraft. Over 800 were flying by 1940 and another 10,000 were built for use in the Second World War. Many of these are still carrying passengers in Britain and other parts of the world today.

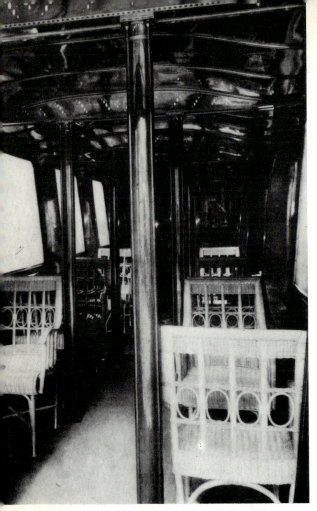

Airships

While aeroplanes were developing, another form of air travel was also being used. Ever since the Montgolfier balloons of the 18th century, there had been great interest in ballooning as a possible form of transport. Hydrogen balloons could travel quite a long way but, like other balloons, could only go where the wind blew them. Experiments began at the end of the 19th century to build a passenger-carrying balloon which could be steered.

Zeppelins

In 1900 in Germany, Count von Zeppelin built a fabric-covered aluminium framework 127 metres long. It enclosed a row of large hydrogen balloons and also had two engines, rudders at the tail and a passenger cabin under the middle. This type of lighter-than-air craft with a strong framework, was called a rigid airship or *dirigible*.

Zeppelin later founded the airline Delag using the dirigible LZ.7 *Deutschland*, which cruised at 60 km per hour. In 1910, it carried a total of 436 passengers between German cities when conventional aeroplanes could only just fly, let alone carry passengers.

Above: the interior of the famous dirigible LZ.7 *Deutschland*. Notice the polished inlaid wood and the light wicker chairs.

Below: the British airship R101 at its mooring mast at Cardington in Bedfordshire, in 1929.

Above: the *Hindenburg* exploding at its mooring mast in May 1937.

British rigid airships

In 1918, Britain built two rigid airships, the *R33* and the *R34*. The R34 made history in 1919 by crossing the Atlantic to New York in 108 hours and returning home in only 75. By the late 1920s, rigid airships became extremely popular for long-distance travel. The *R100*, which was over 233 metres long, made a successful flight to Canada and back in 1930 driven by six 680 cv petrol engines but the *R101* which used five diesel engines, crashed near Paris at the start of a journey to India. Most of the passengers and crew died in the flames and wreckage and the disaster so horrified everyone that Britain, France and the USA refused to build any more rigid airships.

Famous German dirigibles

Airships continued, however, to be built in Germany. The most famous and successful was the five-engined *Graf Zeppelin* which was 236 metres long. In nine years, it flew one and a half million km and carried 13,000 passengers.

A sister ship, the *Hindenburg* began trans-Atlantic crossings in 1936, usually carrying 50 passengers. In 1937, the highly inflammable hydrogen caught fire while the airship was moored at Lakehurst in New Jersey and 36 people died in the flames. This new disaster shocked everyone so much that all commercial airship services immediately ended.

Over the Atlantic

The ambition of many early aviators was to fly across the Atlantic and attempts to do so began after the First World War.

Eastward flights

In the early days of flying, aeroplanes could normally carry only just enough petrol for the 4,800 km journey westwards across the Atlantic from Europe. If one ran out of fuel, it would crash. However, if an aircraft flew from west to east, it could fly with the help of the prevailing westerly wind, which is the one which normally blows across the Atlantic. It would then reach the safety of dry land more quickly. Even today, it is quicker to fly from New York to London than the other way round because of the westerly wind.

The American flying-boat *NC-4* was the first to fly across the Atlantic, in 1919. It made stops in the Azores and Portugal and reached England in 15 days. The first machine to fly direct non-stop was a British Vickers Vimy, flown by the Englishmen Alcock and Brown. They flew through storms and fog, often only just above the water and landed in an Irish bog $16\frac{1}{2}$ hours after taking off from Newfoundland.

Alone across the ocean

Eight years later, a young American called Charles Lindbergh flew across the Atlantic in his Ryan monoplane *Spirit of St Louis*. He flew from New York to Paris and landed in the dark after $33\frac{1}{2}$ hours alone in his tiny cockpit. Thousands of people crowded round to cheer him.

Westward flights

The first flight from Europe, against the west wind, was by the Junkers W.33 *Bremen*, a German monoplane with a huge petrol tank. It started from Ireland in April 1928 and crash-landed on the ice on an island off Labrador in Canada. The first experimental airline flights over the North Atlantic between England and the USA began in June 1937 when two four-engined flying-boats, Imperial Airways' *Caledonia* and Pan American Airways' *Clipper III* crossed in opposite directions to and from New York.

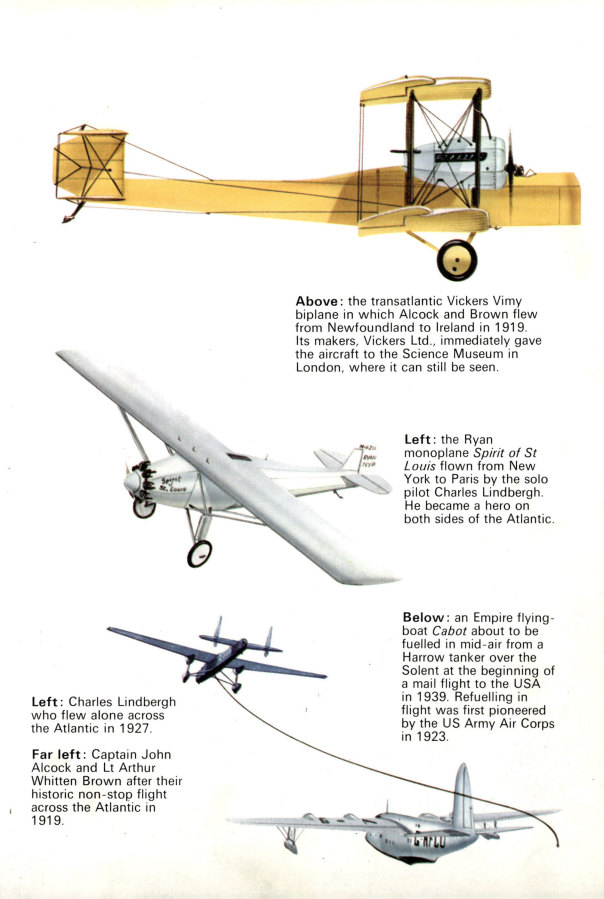

Above: the transatlantic Vickers Vimy biplane in which Alcock and Brown flew from Newfoundland to Ireland in 1919. Its makers, Vickers Ltd., immediately gave the aircraft to the Science Museum in London, where it can still be seen.

Left: the Ryan monoplane *Spirit of St Louis* flown from New York to Paris by the solo pilot Charles Lindbergh. He became a hero on both sides of the Atlantic.

Below: an Empire flying-boat *Cabot* about to be fuelled in mid-air from a Harrow tanker over the Solent at the beginning of a mail flight to the USA in 1939. Refuelling in flight was first pioneered by the US Army Air Corps in 1923.

Left: Charles Lindbergh who flew alone across the Atlantic in 1927.

Far left: Captain John Alcock and Lt Arthur Whitten Brown after their historic non-stop flight across the Atlantic in 1919.

Across the Pacific

After the first successful Atlantic crossings, airmen wanted to cross the Pacific, which is the world's largest ocean. Four small US Army biplanes flew across a narrow part of the ocean between Alaska and Japan in 1924 but they could not carry enough fuel to fly across the widest part. In 1928, a Fokker monoplane *Southern Cross* made the attempt. It still had to land at the tiny islands of Hawaii and Fiji to re-fuel.

The first Pacific flight

Piloted by Charles Kingsford Smith, the *Southern Cross* took off from Oakland, USA on 31 May 1928 to fly the 3,851 km to the first of these distant islands. There was a co-pilot, Charles Ulm, on board to work out the route that the aircraft would take. He checked the course using a compass and radio communication throughout the flight. At night, he used the stars to check his route. After the crew had been in the air for 27 hours, Ulm saw Hawaii and the aircraft was able

to come down safely. Had the co-pilot made one mistake in his calculations, the machine might have missed Hawaii. It would then have been lost at sea when it ran out of fuel.

From Hawaii to Fiji is more than one and a half times the width of the Atlantic but the crew steered the monoplane to a second safe landing after spending over 24 hours in the air. Battling through thunderstorms, Kingsford Smith and his crew reached Brisbane on June 9, completing the very first flight across the Pacific. In September, *Southern Cross* made the first flight over the Tasman Sea from Australia to New Zealand.

A faster Pacific flight

Charles Kingsford Smith, who was later knighted for his long flights, hoped that passenger airliners would soon fly across the Pacific. To prove that the crossing could be made quickly, he set off from Brisbane in 1934 and reached Oakland in only $52\frac{1}{2}$ hours.

The Pacific airlines begin

Sir Charles' dream of a Pacific passenger service came true in 1935 when big Martin Clipper flying-boats came into service. They carried 12 passengers in comfortable cabins from the USA to the Philippine Islands, a distance of 12,875

Below: *Lady Southern Cross,* the aircraft in which Sir Charles Kingsford Smith flew from Brisbane in Australia to Oakland near San Francisco, USA, in 1934.

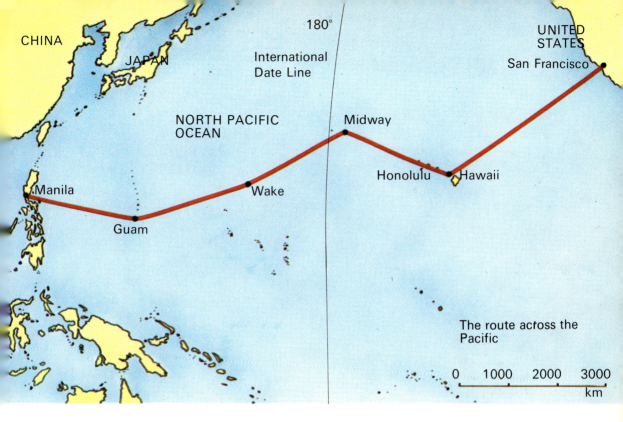

CHINA
JAPAN
180°
International
Date Line
UNITED
STATES
San Francisco
NORTH PACIFIC
OCEAN
Midway
Manila
Wake
Honolulu   Hawaii
Guam

The route across the
Pacific

0   1000   2000   3000
km

km. The flying-boats came down to re-fuel at the islands of Hawaii, Midway, Wake and Guam.

The International Date Line

Clippers flying westwards from Midway on (for example) Saturday mornings crossed a line called the International Date Line. This is an imaginary line. It marks the point where day begins and follows the path of the sun to the west. When the Clippers crossed it, they lost a day because by the time they reached Guam it was already Sunday afternoon! Airline timetables had to be altered. However, passengers gained a day when the Clippers flew eastwards.

Below: a Sikorsky S-42 Flying Clipper, used on the Pacific route by Pan American Airways System.

Air travel in war

Aircraft were used very extensively for battles and bombing during the Second World War. Many technological improvements that later helped passenger aircraft were first used for military aircraft which had to be very fast and which had to carry heavy loads of bombs. The first British and German jet aircraft were used in 1944.

By 1940, most of Europe had been captured by Germany. Britain was cut off from contact with her European allies although some Dutch KLM airliners escaped to Britain and helped to fly important passengers and mail in and out. Crews of KLM and the new British Overseas Airways Corporation flew bravely in dangerous conditions to take necessary supplies where they were needed. They carried no weapons and although the aircraft were camouflaged with green and brown paint to blend with the countryside, many were shot down.

The Horseshoe Route

Great risks were taken by BOAC flying-boats as they crossed Europe by night without lights, on their way to India, Australia, New Zealand and South Africa. After 1940, when Italy joined the war, the flying-boats could no longer cross the Mediterranean without being attacked. A different way had to be found. The service from South Africa was joined at Cairo to the main route to Australia. This formed a great horseshoe-shaped airway from Durban to Sydney along which important officers, official

Left: a BOAC A.W. Whitley V in wartime camouflage. These aircraft were used for flying military supplies and fighter pilots from Gibraltar to Malta by night in 1942.

Right: a Catalina flying-boat, used from 1943 to 1945 by Qantas pilots on the 28-hour crossing from Ceylon to Australia.

Below: a BOAC Boeing 314 in wartime colours.

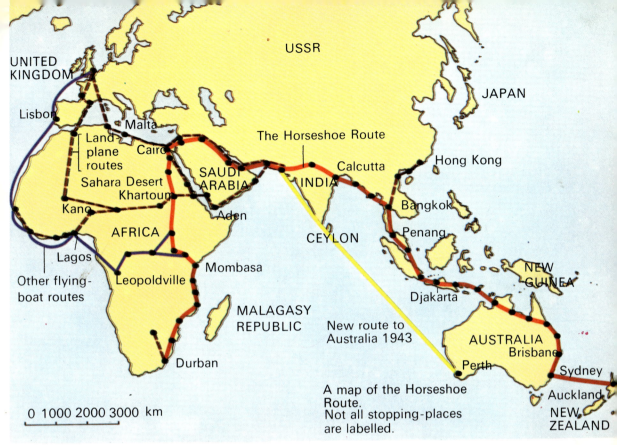

UNITED KINGDOM
Lisbon
Malta
Land-plane routes
Cairo
Sahara Desert
Khartoum
Kano
AFRICA
Lagos
Other flying-boat routes
Leopoldville
Durban
USSR
The Horseshoe Route
SAUDI ARABIA
Aden
INDIA
Calcutta
JAPAN
Hong Kong
Bangkok
Penang
CEYLON
Mombasa
MALAGASY REPUBLIC
New route to Australia 1943
Djakarta
NEW GUINEA
AUSTRALIA
Brisbane
Perth
Sydney
Auckland
NEW ZEALAND

A map of the Horseshoe Route.
Not all stopping-places are labelled.

0 1000 2000 3000 km

papers and war goods could be sent to 16 countries.

Britain was next connected to the Horseshoe Route. Flying-boats were stripped of furnishings so that they could carry more petrol and passengers. They flew for 10,000 km along Atlantic beaches to West Africa. Here, they turned east along the Congo river and joined the Horseshoe at Lake Victoria. Other British aeroplanes joined it at Khartoum after taking a short cut across the Sahara desert.

The secret route to Sweden

Fine ball bearings were made in Sweden and every British aircraft ship and tank needed them. Sweden was surrounded by the enemy and the only way to get the ball bearings was to fly them out secretly by night. Enemy fighters could not catch BOAC's fast aircraft which returned early each morning carrying ball bearings.

The 'Double Sunrise'

When the Japanese entered the war they cut off the Horseshoe route near Australia. In 1943 however, pilots of the Australian airline Qantas found another route. During the next two years, they flew slow Catalina flying-boats over the longest ocean crossing in the world, 4,800 km from Ceylon (now Sri Lanka) to Australia. As much as seven tonnes of petrol was used on each trip and only three passengers were carried. Flights lasted more than 28 hours and so the passengers saw the sun rise twice. For fun, they were made members of the 'Rare and Secret Order of the Double Sunrise'.

25

How an aeroplane flies

Above: a diagram to show air flowing above and below an aerofoil. Air going over the curved upper surface has farther to go than that underneath. It must travel faster and causes a drop in pressure. This creates the upward suction, or lift.

Below: a diagram to show an aerofoil which has lost speed because it climbed too steeply. The smooth airflow over it has been broken, all lift has been lost and the aerofoil has stalled.

Gravity is the force which makes objects fall towards the earth. In order to fly, an aircraft must overcome the force of gravity. It does this both by the shape of its wings and by its speed. When it travels forward, the flow of air over the wings produces an upward force called *lift*. As the aircraft travels faster, the lift increases until it is greater than the aircraft's total weight. At this point, the aeroplane will rise into the air.

The force which makes the aeroplane move forwards is called *thrust*. It can be provided either by propellers or by jet engines. As the aircraft moves forwards, it meets resistance from the air which slows it down. This resistance is called *drag*. The engines must produce enough thrust or speed to overcome drag.

Wing sections

A vertical slice out of a wing, or *aerofoil*, is called the wing section. An aerofoil is cambered or curved at the top. It usually has a blunt front or leading edge and a sharp rear or trailing edge. This shape is chosen so that air moving over the aerofoil travels faster than the air moving under it. As air moves faster, its pressure drops. The pressure of air above the wing is less than that below it and this causes an upward suction which gives the wing most of its lift.

How lift can be lost

An aeroplane stays in the air if it has sufficient speed. If it climbs too steeply and the speed is not increased, the smooth airflow over the wing is broken. Suction is lost and the wing is said to

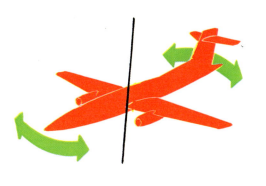

Left: YAWING. When the pilot presses his left rudder pedal, the aeroplane yaws (changes direction) to the left. The right pedal causes it to yaw (or turn) to the right.

Below: ROLLING. A slight turn on the control wheel moves one aileron up and the other down. One wing goes up and the other down. This is called rolling.

Above: PITCHING. By pushing his control wheel forward, the pilot causes the nose of the aircraft to pitch (or move) down and it dives. A backward pull makes it pitch up and the aircraft climbs.

Above: diagrams to show the three ways in which an aeroplane can change its attitude or position in the air.

have stalled. The aeroplane then dives steeply. The speed at which this happens is the *stalling speed*.

Controlling the aeroplane

An aeroplane must be able to turn left and right, to climb and to descend. These movements are controlled by the pilot's feet which rest on the *rudder* pedals and also by his hands which control a wheel. The pedals make the aeroplane turn but can also cause it to skid or slip sideways like a racing car on a corner. This is prevented by a slight turn of the wheel which banks or tilts the wing by moving small *ailerons*, which are wing-like control surfaces. When the pilot wants to climb, he pulls gently on the wheel to raise an elevator or flap hinged to the tailplane, which is the horizontal part of the tail. The airflow pushes the tail down and the nose rises. The pilot pushes the wheel to lower the nose and make the aircraft descend.

A modern airliner

Most modern aircraft have powerful jet engines. When jet fuel or kerosene is burned inside the engine, a jet of hot gases is produced. As this jet of gases shoots backwards, the engine is thrust forwards and this gives the aircraft its speed and power.

Jet engines were first used for warplanes during the Second World War. The first jet passenger aircraft was the British Comet which came into service in 1952 and reached speeds of 790 km per hour. It carried 44 passengers whereas some modern jets can carry more than ten times that number.

The parts of an airliner

The main body of an aircraft is called the *fuselage*. This is a large metal tube which carries the passengers, cargo and the crew, who sit in a flight deck in the nose or tip. Numerous dials show the captain and crew their speed, height, and direction, as well as how the engines are running. Levers control the engines and raise and lower the undercarriage beneath the aircraft. Rows of switches for radio and electrical equipment are built into the roof above the captain and crew.

There is a door which leads from the flight deck into the passenger area. The galley or kitchen and toilets are usually in the tail section although in a very large jet aircraft, there will be more than one galley and of course several lavatories.

At the rear of the fuselage are the *tailplane* and *fin*. These give stability or steadiness in flight. The elevator and rudder, which are used for changing height and direction, are hinged to them.

The wing or *mainplane* is usually made in one section. Inside it, there are huge tanks for fuel and also control rods with which the captain moves the ailerons,

Below: a view from below of a Swissair DC-8. You can see the landing wheels, slats, flaps and ailerons clearly, as well as the engines.

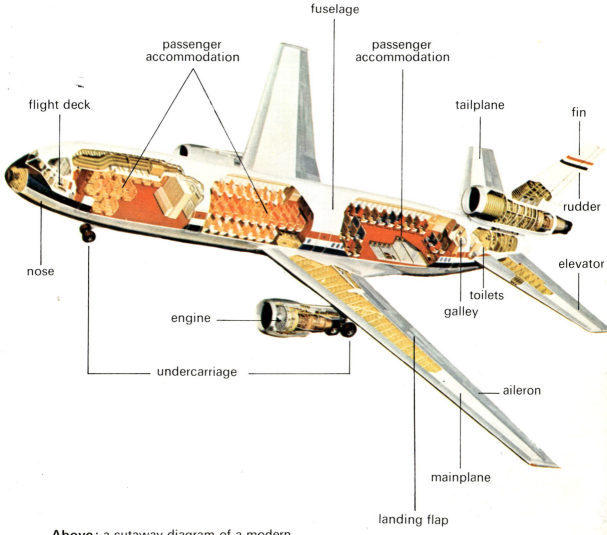

fuselage

passenger
accommodation

passenger
accommodation

flight deck

tailplane

fin

nose

rudder

elevator

engine

toilets

galley

undercarriage

aileron

mainplane

landing flap

Above: a cutaway diagram of a modern
airliner to show the main parts, the
engines and the passenger
accommodation.

slats and flaps. Jet engines are usually
mounted in or below the wing but they
may also be mounted at the tail.

An aircraft is supported on the ground
by its *undercarriage*. This is a structure
carrying the landing wheels. In flight,
the undercarriage retracts or folds away
so that there is less drag. The main wheels
fold away into the wing while the nose
wheel folds up under the flight deck.

Types of airliners

Above: the insignia of Delta Airlines, USA.

Below: the insignia of New Zealand National Airways Corporation.

NAC

Above: the insignia of South African Airways.

Right: a Boeing 707, the first jet airliner built in the USA.

Before 1952 when the first jet passenger aircraft was used, passenger aircraft were driven by petrol engines with propellers. A few, such as the Douglas DC-3, are still in use today.

Aircraft with two jets
The smallest jet liners have two engines and can carry enough fuel to fly for about 2,500 km. They can seat 90 to 172 passengers. The first to be used, in 1959, was the French Caravelle.

Aircraft with three jets
Types of jets with three engines at the rear are usually used for long journeys of over 3,000 km. There is one engine on each side of the tail and one at the top. The most common of these types is the Boeing 727. Over 1,500 have been built and nearly every big airline in the world owns some. British Tridents and Russian Tu-154s have been built along very similar lines. The Trident was the first airliner to make a fully automatic landing during a passenger flight in 1965.

Aircraft with four jets
America's first jet liner was the Boeing 707, built in 1954. It had four engines under its wing and was originally designed to replace propeller aircraft for trans-Atlantic flights.

Other jet liners with four engines are the Boeing 747, the British Airways VC-10 (which has its engines at the rear rather than under the wing), the American DC-8 and the Russian Il-62. When you see aircraft overhead, try to spot where the engines are and how many each airliner has.

Left: the Vickers VC-10 has four jet engines mounted at the rear. First used on the world routes of BOAC, these aircraft now fly with British Airways and carry up to 163 passengers.

Right: first used by British European Airways and later by British Airways, the Hawker Siddeley Trident has three jet engines mounted at the tail. It went into service in 1964 and carries up to 179 passengers.

Left: a Tupolev Tu-154 flown on the routes of the Soviet airline Aeroflot. It too has three jet engines at the rear.

Right: the McDonnell-Douglas DC-9 has two jet engines at the rear. This one belongs to the Swiss airline Swissair. It was built in the USA and can seat up to 172 passengers. This type is used in large numbers all over the world.

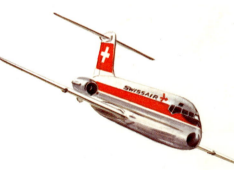

Left: the Dutch Fokker Fellowship is a small jet airliner which can carry up to 65 passengers on short journeys of less than 1,600 kilometres.

Navigation in the air

The earliest pilots did their own navigation. They followed maps and important landmarks such as railways, rivers and coasts, but often went off their course. As air travel distances increased and as aircraft became more powerful, a more precise form of navigation was needed so that aircraft followed a set route.

The direction that an aircraft must follow can be found from a map but the wind nearly always makes the aircraft drift off course. The 'true' direction has to be worked out by the navigator, taking into account the speed of the aeroplane and the speed and direction of the wind. This is called *dead reckoning*. However, he still has to look out for landmarks. At night, he has to check his position by the stars or the glow of towns.

Radio navigation

As accurate navigation became more highly developed, aircraft were able to travel more easily under difficult conditions. By 1934, radio beacons were being built along some air routes. These helped pilots and their crews to find their way when above cloud and unable to see the ground. The beacons sent out radio signals which caused a needle on a dial in the aircraft to point the way from beacon to beacon. When the aircraft reached its destination, it could descend safely through cloud, guided by the voice of a ground controller in the captain's headphones.

Modern navigation

A similar system is used today but radio charts take the place of maps. These are diagrams of airways, which are straight paths in the air, 16 km wide and marked out by beacons. There are airways to all parts of the world and they are 'one-way' to avoid the possibility of a collision. Jet trails which you sometimes see making a criss-cross pattern in the sky form a giant airways diagram.

A navigator also uses DME which stands for Distance Measuring Equipment. This is a radio which shows on a

Below: the principle of dead reckoning. If no allowance is made for the wind (shown by arrows), the aircraft is blown off course along the curved track. By taking the speed and direction of the wind into account, a course can be steered which brings the aircraft straight to its proper destination.

dial the number of kilometres to the next beacon. The pilot can then mark his exact position on a radio chart. Navigation in giant jet aircraft is done by a small computer on board. It works out the course automatically, without the need for radio beacons.

Radar

Radar detects objects by bouncing radio waves off them. Air traffic controllers use radar to space out air traffic at airports at different time intervals and flight levels, for greater safety. Airways are marked on the radar screens and the airliners appear as bright moving dots. Air traffic controllers all over the world use English to talk to pilots of arriving and departing aircraft. This is to avoid misunderstandings or problems in communication, which could be highly dangerous.

Airliners also carry radar. This is used to give precise height above ground and can also detect bad weather ahead, so that the pilot can change his course.

Above: the navigator of a DC-8 calculating the route. He is sitting behind the captain on the flight deck.

Below: aircraft approaching an airport, following specified airways and flying at different levels to avoid any chance of a collision. You can also see the navigation beacons. The buildings and beacons would normally be spread over a far wider area than is shown in this diagram.

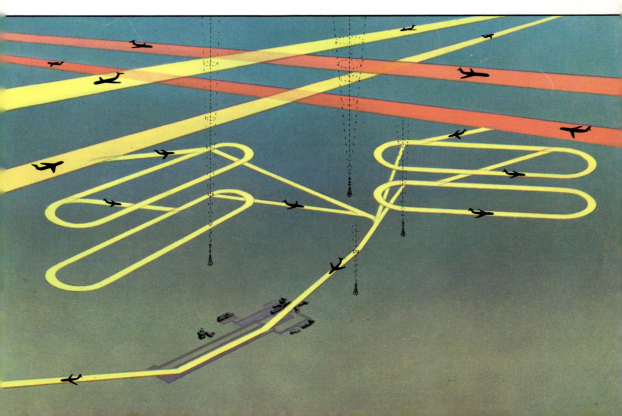

Airports

At a busy international airport such as London/Heathrow's terminal, more than 80,000 passengers may arrive and depart on any day. Most airports are usually fairly close to big cities. However, because aircraft take off and land every few minutes, people living nearby can be seriously disturbed by noise. Airports need a vast space for runways, airport buildings, hangars, servicing areas, car parking, freight loading and storage and customs-warehouses. If new airports are built away from residential areas, land used for farming sometimes has to be built on and this can deprive a large number of farmers of their jobs.

Runways

Modern airliners which can weigh as much as 370 tonnes and land at 270 km per hour need long hard runways for both landing and taking off. The main runway faces the prevailing wind but there are others for use when the wind changes. For safety, the airport buildings have to be well away from the runways. Firemen and ambulances are on duty near the runways 24 hours a day.

Servicing the aircraft

Arriving aircraft are guided to parking places by marshallers, men carrying orange bats. After the passengers have landed, tankers pump thousands of litres

Above: Narita Airport in Japan has been the scene of angry protests from local farmers whose land was taken away.

of jet fuel into the tanks, ready for the next flight. At regular intervals, a powerful tractor tows each airliner to a hangar where engineers carefully inspect every part. All faulty items and even complete engines must be changed before the airliner can fly again.

Airport security

In the past, terrorists have entered aircraft cockpits during flights and threatened the pilots at gun-point, sometimes taking passengers as hostages. It is vitally important to protect both passengers and crew from danger or attack. If a gun were fired or a bomb exploded, the airliner could crash and many people would be killed. Passengers and their luggage are therefore carefully searched before each flight to make sure that no bombs or weapons are carried aboard. Security guards use X-ray machines and metal detectors.

The control tower

High above the terminal is the control tower. Inside, air traffic controllers give permission for flights to take off and land. Approach controllers watch arriving aircraft on radar and steer them safely towards the runway. At busy times or in bad weather, airliners circle round a radio beacon about 15 km away, one above the other at a distance of 300 metres. When the bottom one lands, they all move down 300 metres. This is called *stacking*.

Travelling by jet

There are two sorts of flights, charter flights and scheduled flights. A scheduled flight follows a regular timetable but you are likely to fly by charter aircraft if you take a package holiday. The advantage of a charter flight is that fares are lower than on a scheduled flight. This is because the flight has been specially organized for holiday-makers on condition that the seats are sold well in advance, and that none remain empty.

Boarding

When you have checked in and your baggage has been weighed and inspected, your flight departure is announced. You either walk to the waiting aircraft through the terminal building or are taken there in an airport bus. After you have found a seat, you fasten your seat-belt, ready for take-off.

Emergency equipment

Before take-off, the crew show you the emergency exits. They tell you where the life-jackets and rubber dinghies are and demonstrate how an oxygen mask will drop into your lap if more air is needed.

Take-off

After the doors are shut, the pilot drives bumpily along the ground to the main runway. This is called *taxying*. The air traffic controller then gives clearance or permission for take-off. After about 45 seconds of fast movement on the ground with the engines roaring, the nose goes up and the airliner climbs away steeply. For most people this is a thrilling moment even if they feel a little nervous. Some people feel their ears pop as the altitude changes. A very few people feel airsick. There are glimpses of the countryside below (often at strange angles) before the aircraft seems to hang in the sky with no sensation of movement. The whine of the jet engines can scarcely be heard in the cabin.

Cruising

When the aircraft reaches its cruising height of about 10,000 metres, it flies level at a speed of about 900 km per hour. It is tiring to fly heavy aircraft on long journeys, so the pilot switches on the *automatic pilot*. This works the controls

igℎ
oods
are no
port
and
ser
U
i

Above: this is what the countryside, the coastline and a town look like, seen from an airliner.

Left: during your flight, a snack or meal may be served. Pre-packed trays of food are loaded into the galley and then handed round by the stewardesses.

Far left: a glimpse inside the flight deck of a DC-8. You can see the pilot's radio chart in front of him. The co-pilot is checking the route with the navigator.

and keeps the aircraft in steady flight until it is time to descend.

Descent

Airliners start to descend on a long flight when they are about 300 km from their destination. The captain begins a gradual descent until he is about 15 km from the runway. Then the engine note changes. Slats and flaps move out on the wing to prevent the plane from stalling as it lands. There are thuds under the floor as the undercarriage is lowered ready for landing and you may feel a rumble as the jet touches down on the runway. The engines then roar loudly. This is because the captain has reversed the engine thrust to slow the aircraft down until it finally stops.

...hters

...or freight are heavy to carry and ...rmally needed in a hurry. Trans-...by road and rail is efficient but slow ...air freight is the fastest way of ...ding goods to where they are needed. ...ntil the Second World War, however, ...was difficult to load bulky freight into aircraft and very heavy goods could not be carried easily.

By 1945, large propeller aircraft could transport heavy machinery and even ships' propellers. They were loaded with difficulty through a small door but still arrived at their destinations abroad far more rapidly than by boat and train.

Carrying bigger loads

After 1946, new freight aircraft were built with doors in the nose. Crates could be wheeled up a slope into the fuselage and vehicles could be driven straight in. Some freighters carried up to five cars at a time. CL-44 freighters built in 1960 had tails which swung aside so that freight could be loaded easily from the rear.

Today, jet freighters can lift over 110 tonnes at a time. Goods of all sorts are regularly transported by air. Fish, meat, flowers and fruit can be flown to markets hundreds of kilometres away while still fresh, although deep frozen foods are also carried by air. Cargoes often include urgent medicines and drugs as well as spare parts for machinery.

'Jumbo' freighters

Boeing 747 'Jumbo' freighters have doors in the nose and can carry as much as 110 tonnes of cargo. Inside the hold there is room for a houseful of furniture,

Below: the vast hold of a Boeing 747 Jumbo freighter. Heavy machinery can be shifted by the loaders from one rail to another simply by touching a switch.

Below right: small aircraft being loaded into a Jumbo freighter through doors in the nose.

a team of racing cars and even a small aircraft or yacht. Watches, clocks, precious stones and other small cargo are first packed in specially shaped containers which then run into the hold on rollers.

Animals that fly

The kindest way of sending animals on long journeys is by air. They can usually be transported to zoos or safari parks in only a few hours, carried in large boxes with ample food and water. Baby giraffes, birds and fish, lions, chimpanzees, snakes and even insects are cared for before and after the flight by special nurses.

Air taxis

Air taxis are often hired by businessmen in a hurry or by hospitals transferring sick patients. These are small aircraft with about eight seats. They can use small airfields rather than airports to take

Above: a typical air taxi, used in Ibiza to carry passengers to and from the Spanish mainland. It is a Navajo, which seats about eight passengers.

off and land and are therefore more practical than larger aircraft. Big companies sometimes send executives to meetings abroad or at other factories in small jets. They travel so smoothly at 750 km per hour that secretaries can type letters in flight.

Helicopters

Although small aircraft such as air taxis need only a short runway for taking off and landing, they still need to use an airfield. Helicopters need neither runways nor airfields. They can take off and land vertically almost anywhere and they can also hover and fly sideways. Their top flying speed is only about 320 km per hour, far less than that of an ordinary aircraft, but they can be used almost anywhere. Helicopters were developed just before and during the Second World War and have been widely used since for jungle warfare. The chief helicopter experimenters before 1939 were Focke in Germany and Sikorsky in the USA.

How a helicopter flies

A helicopter is lifted into the air by its *rotor*. This is made up of several blades – large helicopters may have five or seven. The rotor acts in the same way as the propeller and wings of an ordinary aircraft. It provides the power to drive the helicopter along and also lifts the helicopter off the ground. Each blade is like a long narrow aeroplane wing and the helicopter can therefore be called a rotating wing aircraft. It is also a vertical take-off machine since it leaves the ground without needing a forward run.

When the main rotor spins round, the fuselage of the helicopter tends to spin in the opposite direction. To prevent this reaction, a small vertical rotor is fitted to the tail which produces enough force or thrust to balance the fuselage and keep it still. The pilot can then control the helicopter by tilting the main rotor in the direction required. If it is tilted backwards for example, the helicopter will fly backwards. When the rotor is level, the helicopter rises or hovers according to the amount of engine power used by the pilot.

Below: a helicopter preparing to land on an ice floe in Greenland to pick up waiting passengers. It would be impossible to land a conventional aircraft in such conditions. Helicopters are widely used in areas which are isolated.

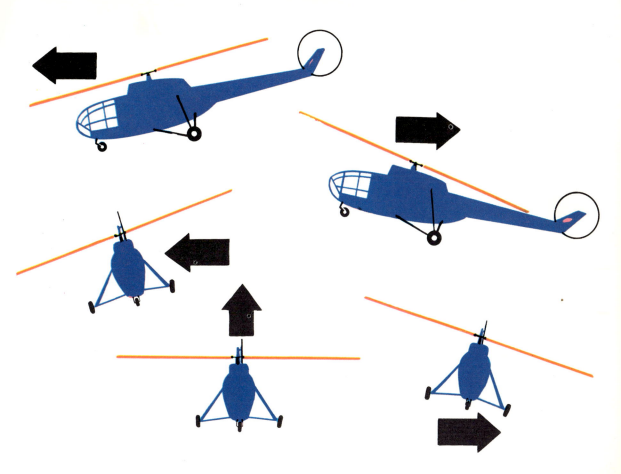

Helicopter uses

As well as being used for fighting fires, rescuing people, spraying crops and for certain kinds of warfare, helicopters are also widely used as air taxis. They can pick up and land passengers even in a car park. Landing areas are marked by a white square round a large letter H. These are called *helipads*. Bigger ones, as at Battersea in London, are called *heliports*. In New York, there are heliports on top of some skyscrapers.

Helicopters are also used on some short air routes between islands and for ferrying crews out to helipads on oil rigs at sea. They are not, however, used for long-distance transport because of their slowness and short range.

Above: a helicopter flies in the direction in which the main rotor is tilted, indicated here by black arrows.

Below: light aircraft, although not as versatile as helicopters, can use airfields for landing instead of airports. They normally have a single engine and carry the pilot and one or two passengers.

Jumbo jets and Concorde

New large passenger jets have been built recently which weigh over 360,000 kg fully loaded. The most famous of these is the Boeing 747 which can seat 490 passengers. Other types of 'Jumbo' jet are the Airbus (296 passengers), the DC-10 (345) and the TriStar (400). They have up to 18 landing wheels to prevent existing runways from cracking under their colossal weight. Passengers travel in wide and spacious cabins, and in the nose of a 747 a spiral staircase links the upper and lower decks. More than 20 cabin staff are needed to look after so many passengers.

Jumbo jets can carry a greater number of passengers in fewer journeys than smaller airliners, which makes them very practical. However, many people have feared the consequences of a crash involving a Jumbo since so many people might be killed. In March 1977, these fears became reality when two Jumbo jets collided on the ground at Tenerife airport after one of the pilots misunderstood instructions from air traffic controllers. 575 people were killed in the worst aircraft disaster ever known. There were only 69 survivors out of all the passengers.

Below: the interior of the two-engined European Airbus which can carry 296 passengers in great comfort. The cabin is much wider than that of an ordinary airliner and the stewardesses can circulate easily.

Over 60 Airbuses were in use in 1979 by European airlines as well as by airlines in Korea, the USA, South Africa, Thailand, India and Egypt.

Above: a dramatic shot of Concorde taking off in front of a crowd of spectators at the Farnborough Air Show. In front is an Air France Airbus and, partly hidden behind Concorde, is a TriStar. British Airways have five Concordes for services to Bahrein and to the USA. Air France uses four between Paris, the USA and South America.

Supersonic aircraft

At sea level, sound travels through the air at 1,225 km per hour in standard atmosphere conditions. Aircraft which can travel faster than this are called *supersonic* aircraft. The new Anglo-French airliner Concorde can fly at about 2,175 km per hour and can reach New York from London, a distance of about 5,530 km, in about three and a half hours.

Supersonic aircraft have to be specially designed to pass safely through the *sound barrier*. This is the severe *turbulence* caused by shock waves when an aircraft travels near the speed of sound.

Aircraft of the future

One of the most important developments in aircraft will be VTOL which stands for Vertical Take-Off and Landing. There are already military aircraft such as the Harrier which can take off and land like helicopters but which can travel at far greater speeds. Designers hope one day to build a large jet airliner with VTOL, possibly by the late 1980s. This may mean that airports with long runways will no longer be necessary.

43

Books to read

Famous U.S. Navy Fighter Planes, David C. Cook; Dodd, Mead and Co. 1972

Helicopters and Airplanes of the U.S. Army, Frank J. Delear; Dodd, Mead and Co. 1977

Cleared for Takeoff: Behind the Scenes at an Airport, Charles Coombs; William Morrow 1969

See Inside an Airport, Joseph Rutland; Watts, Franklin 1978

Who Puts the Plane in the Air?, Dina Anastasio; Watts, Franklin 1977

Famous Firsts in Aviation, Jesse Davidson; G.P. Putnam 1974

Your Book of Flying, Denis M. Desoutter; Transatlantic

Great Flying Adventures, Sherwood Harris; Random House 1973

Airport, Arthur Reed; Silver Burdett Company 1978

Aviation Careers, Arnold Madison; Watts, Franklin 1977

The Complete Book of Flying, Lyle K. Engel; School Book Service 1976

Pioneers of Flight, Henry T. Walhauser; Hammond Inc. 1969

Man in Flight: How the Airlines Operate, Creighton Peet; MacRae 1972

Flight, H. Guyford Stever and James J. Haggerty; Time-Life Science Library 1969

By the Seat of Their Pants, Phil Ault, Dodd, Mead and Co. 1978

Flying Aces of World War I, Gene Gurney; Random House 1965

The Illustrated Encyclopedia of Aircraft, David Mondey, ed; A & W Publishers 1978

Places to visit

Why not visit an airport and find out more about air travel? The major American airports are Chicago-O'Hare, Hartsfield (Atlanta), Los Angeles, John F. Kennedy (New York City), San Francisco, Dallas-Fort Worth, LaGuardia (New York City), Stapleton (Denver), Miami, Washington (D.C.), Logan (Boston), Honolulu, Philadelphia, Detroit Metropolitan, and St. Louis. There may also be smaller airports located near your home.

Some of the airplanes mentioned in this book can be seen in museums. Listed below are some American museums that have excellent collections of aircraft as well as interesting exhibits on many aspects of flight:

The Air Museum, Claremont, California

The Experimental Aircraft Air Museum, Hales Corners, Wisconsin

The California Museum of Science and Industry, Los Angeles, California

The Pacific Science Center, Seattle, Washington

The San Diego Aerospace Museum, San Diego, California

The National Air and Space Museum, Washington, D.C.

The Air Force Museum, Dayton, Ohio

Things to do

With field glasses you will be surprised how clearly you can see the aircraft which fly near your home. Learn to recognize small private aircraft and to pick out air taxis, helicopters, propeller and jet-driven aircraft.

Watch for vapour trails passing overhead. Find their direction with a compass and use an atlas to find where the airliners may be going. Some radio sets can be tuned to listen to pilots talking to air traffic controllers.

Remember though that these messages are private, rather like police messages.

Collect pictures of as many types of aircraft as you can.

Collect stamps which show pictures of aircraft.

Glossary

Here is a list of some of the more difficult terms used in this book.

Aerofoil: the specially shaped wing which creates *lift* as it moves quickly through the air.

Ailerons: movable sections on the outer wings. One goes up and the other down to tilt the wing as the aircraft turns.

Automatic pilot: a small machine which relieves the pilot of strain on long flights by keeping the aircraft steady on course.

Biplane: an aeroplane with an upper and a lower wing on each side of the fuselage.

Dead reckoning: working out the aircraft's course mathematically, taking the speed and direction of the wind into account.

Dirigible: an airship which can be steered by means of a rudder.

Drag: air resistance which slows up an aircraft in flight.

Fin: a fixed upright surface at the tail which keeps the aircraft on a straight course.

Fuselage: the main body of an aircraft containing the flight deck, passenger cabin and cargo hold.

Helipad: a small marked space on which a helicopter may land, eg on an oil rig or on private land.

Heliport: a landing space large enough for several helicopters to pick up passengers or freight.

Lift: the upward force which supports the aircraft in the air, made by the wing as it moves quickly through the air.

Mainplane: the largest wing of the aircraft.

Monoplane: an aeroplane with only one wing on each side of the fuselage.

Rotor: the circle of blades which spins above a helicopter to lift it off the ground.

Rudder: a movable control surface hinged to the rear of the fin which enables the pilot to change direction.

Seaplane: an aeroplane with floats, similar to canoes, instead of wheels so that it can alight on water. It differs from a flying-boat which has the hull of a boat instead of a fuselage.

Sound barrier: a common name for the shock wave, heard on the ground as a double boom, when an aircraft reaches the speed of sound.

Stacking: airliners circling one above the other as they wait their turn to land at an airport.

Stalling speed: the speed below which wings cease to produce *lift*. The aircraft then falls.

Subsonic (of an aircraft): flying below the speed of sound.

Supersonic (of an aircraft): flying faster than the speed of sound.

Tailplane: a small wing at the rear which keeps the aircraft in level flight.

Taxying: using the aircraft's engines to drive it along the ground.

Thrust: power from the engines needed to propel the aircraft through the air.

Turbulence: rough, disturbed air which causes the aircraft to rock about in flight.

Undercarriage: an aircraft landing gear made up of struts, wheels, axles and brakes.

Index

Illustrations appear in
bold type